Performance of Face Recognition Algorithms on Compressed Images

NIST Interagency Report 7830

George W. Quinn, Patrick J. Grother

Image Group
Information Access Division
Information Technology Laboratory
National Institute of Standards and Technology

December 4, 2011

1. Table of Contents

2. Introduction

This report provides a comprehensive assessment of the ability of face recognition algorithms to compare compressed standard face images. Six well performing algorithms from the Multiple Biometric Evaluation (MBE) 2010 Still Face Track are used to compare face images compressed in JPEG and JPEG2000 formats. A primary goal of this report is to identify the maximum storage constraints under which verification systems can effectively operate. Toward this end, guidelines and recommendations are provided for the efficient compression and storage of face images for biometric applications.

Many biometric systems operate with restrictions on the size of stored samples. For example, smart-cards (e.g. ePassports and government PIV cards) have a maximum storage capacity for storing their biometric samples. In addition, systems employing limited-bandwidth networks are often bottlenecked by the size of the biometric data they transfer. Although proprietary formats for storing facial features (i.e. matchable templates) are often more compact, their use should be avoided for several reasons. First, their content is non-standard, non-interoperable, and not suitable for cross-agency exchange of data. Second, their widespread adoption would undermine fair competition in the marketplace. Lastly, when the original image is discarded, the human interpretable representation of the face is lost. Discarding the original image in exchange for the proprietary template would also prevent systems from benefiting from inevitable future improvements in the automated feature extraction and template generation process. A way to avoid these pitfalls is to store face images according to open standards such as ISO/IEC 19794-5 [1], FIPS PUB 201-1 [2], ANSI/NIST ITL 2007 [3], and the National Science Technology Council (NSTC) registry.

However, the greater storage requirement of standard face images often necessitates the use of lossy methods of image compression. When lossy compression is applied to a face image, information is selectively discarded in exchange for a more compact representation. At low compression the information loss is negligible, but when compression is applied with sufficient severity, visible artifacts are introduced that detrimentally affect the feature extraction process. Ultimately, the result is a loss in matching accuracy with higher amounts of compression corresponding to greater reductions in accuracy. This report investigates this speed-accuracy trade-off and identifies optimal parameters for compressing face images.

Several methods of reducing the storage requirements of face images are explored, including JPEG and JPEG2000 compression, pixel resolution down-sampling, and color space reduction. Some of these can be applied in tandem. For example, Section 6.3 demonstrates that reducing the pixel resolution prior to applying JPEG compression often results in a performance benefit. Section 6.6 directly compares JPEG and JPEG2000 compression and shows that JPEG2000 does not always provide superior performance. Sections 6.7 and 6.8 investigate the benefit of reducing the color space of images to grayscale. Storing images in grayscale is often feasible since it provides a more compact representation and most matching algorithms are capable of matching grayscale images as well as color.

Some caveats are worth mentioning. First, this report is not intended to compare algorithms or evaluate the latest state-of-the-art of face recognition. This was already done in NISTIR 7709 [4] and other evaluations [5][6]. Additionally, this report does not explore Region of Interest (ROI) encoding, which is supported by the JPEG2000 standard. Finally, only verification (and not one-to-Many) performance is investigated.

2.1. Application Scenarios

Many biometric systems must operate with restrictions on the size of their biometric data. Two broad scenarios addressed in this report are:

1. *Identity credential:* A compressed face image is stored on a space-limited device and compared to a live capture of an uncompressed image. The stored image is captured in a controlled setting during a formal enrollment session (for example, at a consular office). The storage device, possibly an ePassport or government PIV card, has space limitations that necessitate compression of the image. The live image is captured later and exists only for the duration of the verification attempt. Thus, it does not need to be compressed.

2. *Networked System:* A face image is compressed and sent over a bandwidth-limited network to a central location for matching. Compression is required to reduce the transfer time of the image. The enrollment samples at the central location are stored either losslessly or with light compression. An example of this scenario might be when a police officer pulls over an automobile driver and uses a mobile biometric capture device to verify the driver's identity against MVA records

The investigations in this report only address verification scenarios where one of the two compared images is compressed. This excludes one-to-many scenarios (e.g. watch list, database consolidation) where a prior claim to identity is not provided or assumed. For simplicity, we always refer to the compressed images as being in the enrollment set, although this may not always be the case (e.g. in the networked system, the verification samples are compressed).

Note that for the identity credential scenario, a more heavily compressed image would take less time to transfer from the smart card to the system for comparison, which would improve throughput time. Likewise, a more heavily compressed image would transfer more quickly in the networked system scenario.

2.2. Relation to the MBE Still Face Track

This report follows the MBE-STILL Face Track, which is covered by NISTIR 7709 [4]. The MBE-STILL was a large-scale evaluation of the latest state-of-the-art of automated face recognition technology. This report differs in that it does not seek to assess the progress of automated face recognition or to compare algorithm performance. Rather, its primary goal is to investigate the potential for automated matchers to compare compressed face images.

2.3. Prior Studies

Several studies have investigated the ability of matchers to compare compressed face images. Delac et. al. [7] ran several traditional face recognition algorithms (e.g. PCA, LDA) over color images from the FERET database [8] and found that verification accuracy typically begins to drop at a compression ratio of 24:1 (1 bit-per-pixel). They also determined that a mild amount of compression actually improves performance slightly due to its smoothing effects. It is yet to be determined whether the same effect occurs for the latest commercial and academic algorithms. Mascher-Kampfer et. al [9] tested several methods of compression on face and fingerprint images and found JPEG2000 and SPIHT to be superior to JPEG strictly in terms of the Peak-Signal-To-Noise-Ratio (PSNR). However, there is uncertainty with regard to whether PSNR provides an accurate quantitative measure of matching performance. Bourlai et. al. [10] proposed a method of compressing image data for smart card based verification systems (where matching is performed on the smart card itself). The method is limited to the specific scenario in which the compressed face image is uploaded to the smart card for comparison.

While these studies provide a good baseline, they are often limited in scope and tend to use matching algorithms that do not represent the latest state-of-the-art. The datasets used are also fairly small which makes generalizing results difficult. By comparison, this study runs six commercial matching algorithms over thousands of images representing hundreds of individuals. Even conclusions from prior studies on face recognition must sometimes be reaffirmed since recognition algorithms tend to incorporate improvements fairly regularly. The most accurate matching algorithms often achieve an order of magnitude reduction in error rates every few years [4], similar to Moore's Law.

3. Experimental Environment

3.1. Dataset

The dataset used in this study consists of images from the Sandia National Laboratories. They are the same images used for the 2010 MBE-STILL Face Track and the FRVT 2006 and ICE 2006 Large-Scale Results. The images were captured in a controlled setting with a 4 Megapixel Canon PowerShot G2 and have a bit-depth of 24 (8 per color channel). Prior to compressing the images, ground truth eye coordinates were used to scale, rotate, and crop the images to the token format specified in ISO/IEC 19794-5. Token images always place the eye coordinates at a fixed position in the image, as shown in Figure 1.

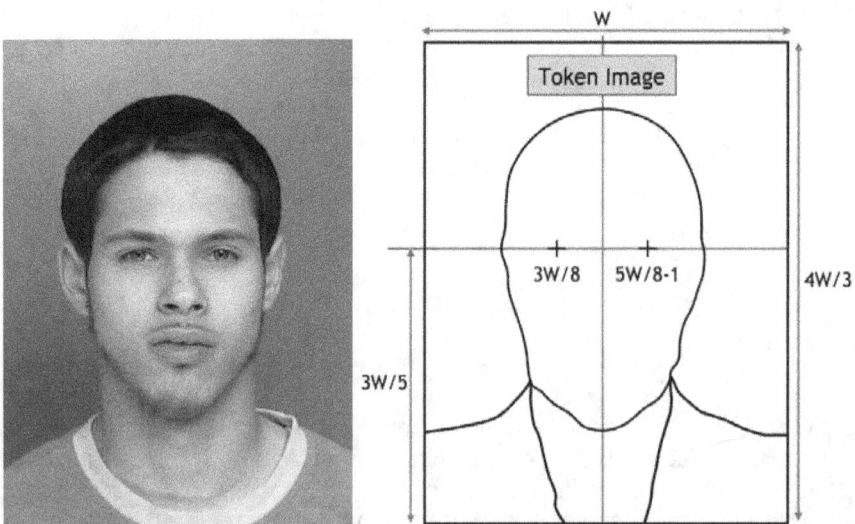

Figure 1. At left, a tokenized image from MEDS-I [11] that is fairly representative of Sandia images. At right, illustration of where eye positions are located in a token image.

Similar to the image shown in Figure 1, controlled Sandia images were captured with a plain background. This improves the ability of JPEG and JPEG2000 to compress the images since large areas of uniform color require less space to encode. When moderate to severe compression is necessary, it is generally good practice to capture images with a uniform and plain background. A less desirable alternative is to mask the background with a uniform color post-capture. The disadvantage of this is that it runs the risk of masking out useful portions of the face, which is especially likely to occur if the eye coordinates were incorrectly localized.

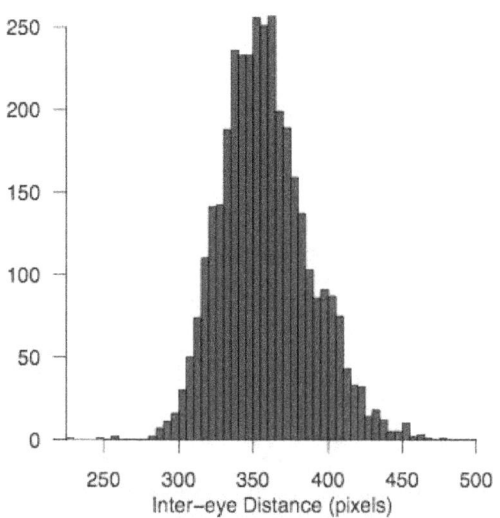

Figure 2. Histogram of eye distances for Sandia images according to one algorithm.

Figure 2 shows a histogram of eye distances for Sandia images. In this study token images were down-sampled to specific inter-eye distances ranging from 16 to 256 pixels. The images almost always had sufficient background area such that the tokenization process never had to sample from regions outside of the original image. Pixels corresponding to areas outside of the original image were assigned a solid color similar to the color of the background. In situations where this problem arises, a good rule of thumb is to assign to such pixels colors that maintain the consistency of the background.

The Sandia images used in this study were originally stored as JPEGs at low compression. Although this is undesirable since it means the images were not uncompressed to begin with, the amount of lossy compression applied is far below what is known to affect recognition accuracy. The JPEGs were converted to uncompressed 24-bit RGB images prior to tokenization.

3.2.   Algorithms

The commercial matching algorithms used this report were originally submissions to the MBE Still Face Track. The date range for submissions was between January 27[h] 2010 and May 14[h] 2010. Throughout this report algorithms are referred to according to their assigned identifiers. Table 1 lists the associations between company and algorithm.

Z20 = Neurotechnology	X20 = Cognitec	V20 = NEC
P20 = PittPatt	W20 = L1 Identity	Y20 = Sagem

Table 1. Identities of algorithm providers.

4. Compression techniques

Several methods of lossy image compression exist. In addition to JPEG and JPEG2000 compression, we also investigate pixel resolution down-sampling and color space reduction. One of our primary goals is to determine the optimal parameters for image compression such that matching accuracy is minimally affected. Note that not all methods of compression are mutually exclusive. For example, JPEG supports several methods of color space reduction, and the pixel resolution of images can be down-sampled prior to applying JPEG or JPEG2000 compression.

4.1. Resolution Downsampling

One of the simplest methods of compressing an image is to down-sample the pixel resolution. This has the obvious effect of discarding the finer details contained in the image. Several prior studies have addressed the problem of matching low-resolution face images [12][13][14][15][16][17]. However, most either focus on specific problems not directly applicable to this evaluation (e.g. using a sequence of images captured in succession to compensate for their low-resolution) or propose new and relatively unproven matching techniques.

In this evaluation, we apply resolution down-sampling in tandem with JPEG and JPEG2000 compression. Our expectation is that optimal size reduction is achieved by performing a down-sampling operation prior to storing the image in one of the two lossy compression formats. We use bilinear interpolation for sub-sampling during the tokenization step. Each token image is scaled to have a fixed number of pixels between the center of the eyes. The ISO/IEC 19794-5 requires token images to have at least 60 pixels between the eyes (based on matching results in the appendix as well as other factors), but for the purposes of our evaluation we down-sample to distances as low as 16.

4.2. JPEG

JPEG enjoys wide support and is used by many government organizations to store face images for potential biometric use. For example, the FBI uses JPEG to store mugshots in IAFIS, and the cameras used by US-VISIT at ports of entry always capture face images as JPEGs. JPEG compresses images in several steps. First, the color space is down-sampled using chroma sub-sampling. Chroma sub-sampling is a method of reducing the space requirements for the color information in a way that minimizes the visual perception of quality loss. It exploits the fact that the eye tends to perceive variations in color less well than changes in luminance. After the color space is reduced, the image is separated into non-overlapping 8-by-8 pixel blocks, sometimes referred to as tiles. If the dimensions of the image are not divisible by 8, a padding is transparently added to the right and/or bottom of the image. In this study token images were always scaled to have a width divisible by 8 to prevent padding in the horizontal direction. The primary lossy compression step for JPEG is applied to each 8-by-8 block separately, which leads to the familiar blocking artifacts found in heavily compressed images. The degree to which the color frequencies are quantized is specified by a JPEG quality value.

Smart-cards and other storage mediums typically have a maximum amount of space available for storing a face image. Since JPEG quality values do not perfectly correspond to file sizes, the best method of reducing a JPEG image's storage requirement to a target size is to apply compression at progressively lower quality values until the target size is achieved. We used the libjpeg software library [18] to compress images in this manner.

4.3. JPEG2000

JPEG2000 was developed to supercede JPEG and uses newer wavelet based technology. Although less widely supported than its predecessor, it has shown promise as a method of storing fingerprint images [19] and standard iris formats [20]. Outside of biometrics, JPEG2000 has demonstrated itself superior to JPEG at compressing images to small sizes [21] in terms of the peak signal-to-noise ratio.

JPEG2000 allows several parameters to be adjusted when compressing an image. For example, it supports arbitrarily defined tile sizes. At first this would seem to introduce an additional dimension to the compression process. However, the tile sizes tend to be quite large (e.g. 1024 x 1024) and their primary purpose is to reduce memory usage when loading large files. Thus, in this evaluation the tile size for JPEG2000 images was always set to the size of the entire image. A second functionality supported by JPEG2000 is region-of-interest (ROI) encoding. This allows the user to specify areas of the image that are deemed more important (e.g. the actual face region). The compression algorithm then assigns greater weight to preserving the features in these areas. Region-of-interest encoding had limited application to this study since the area outside of the face is simply a uniform background, which already consumes a minimal amount of the coding budget. The open source JasPer library [22] was used to encode images in the JPEG2000 format.

4.4. Comparison of JPEG and JPEG2000 Compression Artifacts

JPEG and JPEG2000 both introduce compression artifacts to images at high compression ratios, although the visual appearance of the artifacts differs for the two compression methods. Figure 3 demonstrates the differences by compressing an image from the MEDS-I dataset using JPEG and JPEG2000. The middle image is included for fair comparison and does not demonstrate the compression effects of JPEG2000 as well as the right-most image. As can be seen, JPEG tends to produce "blocking" and "mosquito" noise around areas of sharp contrast while JPEG2000 introduces blurring and ringing artifacts. Note the slight difference in background color between the left image and the two right images images, which indicates that some color distortion is occurring as well.

JPEG at 6000 bytes   JPEG2000 at 6000 bytes   JPEG2000 at 2000 bytes

Figure 3. Comparison of the visual artifacts introduced by JPEG and JPEG2000 on a token image (artifacts may not present themselves well on paper print-outs).

Some face images have properties that make them more difficult to compress. Areas outside of the face region that contain a lot of high frequency information (e.g. cluttered backgrounds, lots of hair) require more space to encode, which takes away from the space available for storing the more relevant features of the face. When possible, face images should be captured against a solid and uniform background.

4.5.   Color Space Reduction

This evaluation investigates different methods of sub-sampling the color space to reduce storage requirements. An obvious method of reducing the color space is to transform the image from color to grayscale, effectively reducing the dimension of the color space from three to one. This is explored for both JPEG and JPEG2000 formats in Section 6.

By default, libjpeg[1] and most other JPEG encoders use 4:2:0 chroma sub-sampling to reduce the color space of the original image. The method begins by separating the image into 2-by-2 pixel blocks. Within each block, all four pixels are assigned the same color and only the luminance component varies. The rationale behind chroma sub-sampling is that the eye is less sensitive to changes in color than it is to variations in brightness. If an image is originally stored as a 24-bit RGB raster, then applying 4:2:0 chroma sub-sampling would reduce the bits-per-pixel from 24 down to 14. An alternative method of color space reduction is 4:4:0 chroma sub-subsampling, which separates the image into 4-by-4 blocks such that the pixels within each block are assigned the same color. This results in a greater reduction in the number of bits-per-pixel (24 down to 9.5), although it comes at a sacrifice of a greater loss in color information. Note that since JPEG compression already performs color space reduction, transforming the image to grayscale will not result in an immediate two-thirds drop in the file size.

JPEG2000 compression separates an image into three color channels and performs a compression operation on each one individually. When JPEG2000 stores an image in grayscale, only one color channel is retained.

Color images were converted to grayscale using the following commonly applied weighted scheme [3][23]:

$$Luminance = 0.30R + 0.59G + 0.11B$$

---

[1] The libjpeg software library is the de-facto standard for storing JPEG images. By default it applies 4:2:0 chroma sub-sampling. Turning off color sub-sampling would require a modification to the source code.

5.   Metrics

The following metrics are used to measure recognition accuracy, and to quantify certain aspects of compression.

5.1.   Compression Ratio

The compression ratio is a measure of the amount of compression applied to an image. Formally, it is defined as

$$\text{compression ratio} = \frac{\text{uncompressed size}}{\text{compressed size}}$$

Higher compression ratios correspond to greater reductions in data size. For face images the uncompressed size of an image, in bits, is its width times its height times its bit depth. Thus, for a given target file size, it is a simple process to compute the compression ratio that would reduce the size of the image to a specific targeted file size.

Higher compression ratios produce smaller file sizes but tend to discard more information. Therefore, if a smart card provides a certain amount of space for storing a face image, it is advantageous to use as much of that storage space as possible. This is easy for JPEG2000 since it allows the compression ratio to be specified during the compression step. JPEG, on the other hand, takes as input a quality value with the property that lower quality values roughly correspond to higher compression ratios. Although the relation is monotonic, it requires the repeated application of progressively lower JPEG quality levels until the target file size is achieved.

For clarity, most figures in this report refer to the target file size rather than the compression ratio. The conversion from target file size to compression ratio is simple given that the uncompressed bit-depth of Sandia images is always 24 (8 for grayscale), and the number of pixels in a token image can be determine from the inter-eye distance.

5.2.   Peak Signal-to-noise ratio

The peak signal-to-noise ratio (PSNR) provides a measure of the degree of corruption introduced to an image when it is compressed. It is defined as

$$\text{PSNR}(I_o, I_c) = 20 \log_{10} \left(\frac{MAX}{RMS(I_o, I_c)} \right)$$

where MAX is the maximum possible value for any pixel, and $RMS(I_1, I_2)$ stands for the root mean square, which is the square root of the average squared difference in pixel values between the original image I_o, and the compressed image I_c. For RGB color images, the squared difference is taken over each color channel

$$RMS(I_o, I_c) = \sqrt{\frac{1}{3wh} \sum_{i=0}^{w-1} \sum_{j=0}^{h-1} \sum_{c=0}^{2} \left[I_o(i,j,c) - I_c(i,j,c) \right]^2}$$

where the last component, c, indexes the color channel (red, green, or blue). The images used for this study were converted to 24-bit RGB, where each 8-bit color channel has a peak value of 255. Higher bit depths (e.g. 16 bits per color channel) were not considered. Higher PSNR values indicate greater fidelity to the original image. Conversely, greater amounts of compression introduce artifacts to the image that lower the PSNR. If the image is perfectly represented in the compressed image (i.e. it is lossless), then the root mean square is zero and the PSNR does not exist.

5.3. Matching Accuracy

Verification accuracy is measured as a trade-off between two types of possible errors. Both are defined below.

False Match Rate (FMR): The rate at which impostor comparisons produce a similarity score above a decision threshold. For the access control scenario, a false match would mistakenly grant access to an unauthorized user. In statistical terms, if the null hypothesis is the claim that the face images being compared are from different subjects when it is true, then the false match rate is the measured probability of a Type I error.

$$FMR(T) = \frac{\text{Number of impostor comparisons with score at or above threshold, T}}{\text{Total number of impostor comparisons}}$$

False Non-match Rate (FNMR): The rate at which genuine comparisons produce a similarity score below a threshold. For the access control scenario, a false non-match would mistakenly reject access to an authorized user. In statistical terms, if the null hypothesis is the claim that the face images being compared are from different subjects when it is false, then the false non-match rate is the measured probability of a Type II error.

$$FNMR(T) = \frac{\text{Number of genuine comparisons with score below threshold, T}}{\text{Total number of genuine comparisons}}$$

Failure to Enroll (FTE): A failure to enroll occurs when the feature extractor fails to find a face in the enrollment image and therefore fails to generate a template that can produce useful comparison scores. It can also occur if the feature extractor elects not to produce a template due, for example, to an extremely poor quality face image. When the feature extractor fails to find a face image in a verification or identification image, the occurrence is known as a Failure to Acquire (FTA). If the face is incorrectly located but a template is still produced, it is not referred to as a failure to enroll.

High compression ratios can introduce visual artifacts to the face image that make it difficult to correctly locate the face. The solution is to localize the eye coordinates and tokenize the face prior to compressing the image. In this study, the API did not support the option to specify the eye coordinates prior to generating a template, although the eye coordinates were always in the same place in the enrollment images.

Failure to Compress (FTC): A failure to compress occurs when the compression algorithm is unable to compress the image to the desired file size. This occurs for JPEG images when, even at the lowest possible quality setting, the file size of the compressed image is still too large to meet the specified criteria. A failure to compress would occur prior to any attempt to create a matchable template from the compressed image.

5.4. Bootstrapping for uncertainty estimation

Bootstrapping is an empirical method of measuring the variability of a statistic, often employed when the variability cannot be determined analytically. In this evaluation bootstrapping is sometimes used to estimate the level of uncertainty of an error statistic (e.g. FNMR) at a fixed threshold. A large number of bootstrap iterations are performed to produce a distribution for the measured statistic. Each bootstrap iteration samples with replacement from the original set of comparisons. Bootstrapping relies on several assumptions, including the assumption that the sample data is iid (independent and identically distributed). However, when different comparisons involve the same individual, the comparisons are likely to be correlated due to the existence of Doddington's zoo [24]. This violation of the independence assumption may result in an underestimation of the variability of the measured statistic for some figures in this report.

6. Investigations

Results of the evaluation are organized into a series of investigations. The first few investigations examine the effect of specific methods of image compression (e.g. JPEG and JPEG2000) on matching accuracy. Some of the latter investigations address issues relating to the overall quality and reliability of a biometric system that must compare compressed face images. At the beginning of each section, the main purpose of the investigation is stated in bold. Findings and recommendations are provided at the end.

6.1. Reducing the Inter-eye Distance

Purpose: To determine the impact of reducing the inter-eye distance on matching accuracy, and to identify the ideal range of inter-eye distances for token face images.

For a token image, reducing the number of pixels between the center of the eyes (i.e. the inter-eye distance) is equivalent to down-sampling the pixel resolution. Fewer pixels means less information needs to be stored, which results in a smaller file size. Figure 4 shows the effect of reducing the inter-eye distance on matching accuracy for all 6 algorithms. Only enrollment images were down-sampled. The figure shows that all algorithms appear to benefit little from inter-eye distances above 96. Although the ISO/IEC 19794-5 standard requires at least 60 pixels between the eyes, two of the algorithms (Z20 and Y20) show higher FNMR at 64 pixels than at 96 pixels. Some algorithms are better capable of handling smaller inter-eye distances than others. The most robust algorithm appears to be V20, which only shows very small increases in FNMR for inter-eye distances all the way down to 24 pixels. P20 appears capable of tolerating small inter-eye distances as well.

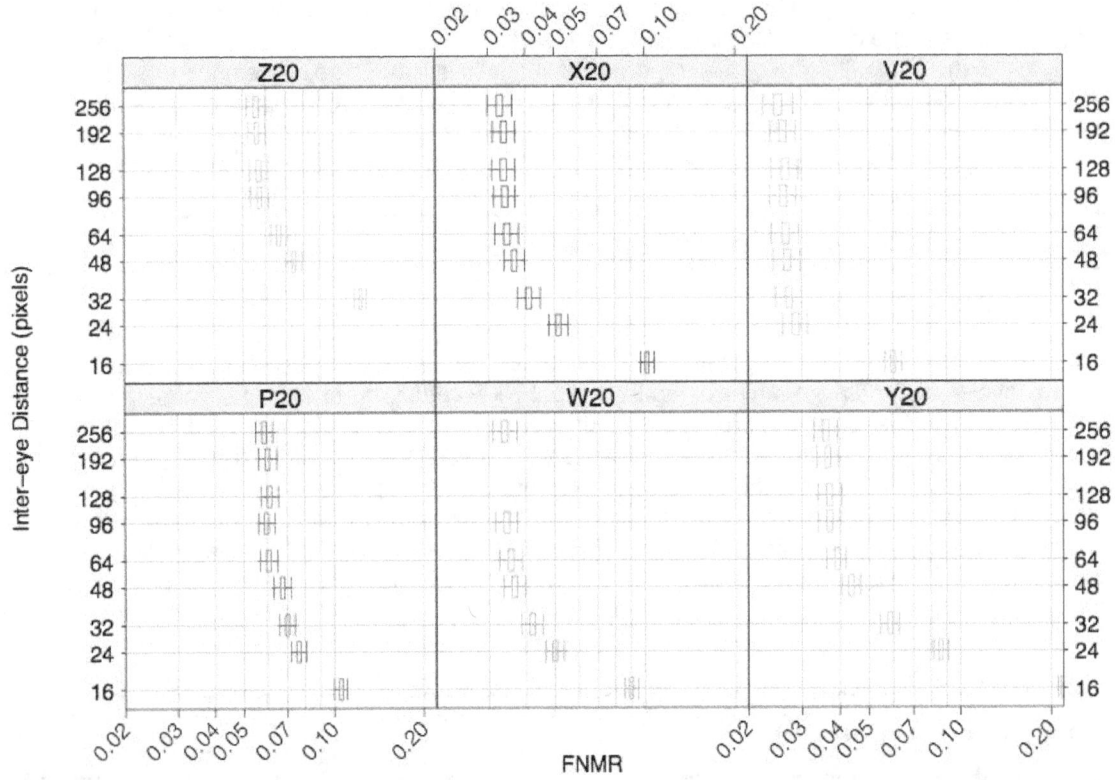

Figure 4. FNMR (at FMR=0.001) as a function of inter-eye distance for 6 algorithms. No JPEG or JPEG2000 compression was applied. Some boxes lie outside the visible range of FNMR.

In Figure 4, the decision threshold was adjusted for each inter-eye distance to elicit an FMR of 0.001. However, face recognition systems must often handle images subjected to varying amounts of compression, and typically a fixed universal decision threshold is applied to all comparisons. The question then becomes whether the higher error rates associated with heavily compressed images translate into a higher FNMR, a higher FMR, or both. The desirable behavior for verification systems is for the impostor distribution to remain stable and predictable. Not only does this allow systems to be easily calibrated to operate at known false math rates, but it renders such systems less vulnerable to accepting false claims of identity when comparing highly compressed images. A system prone to falsely accepting poor quality samples would be susceptible to spoofing by deceptive users.

Figure 5 plots FMR and FNMR as a function of inter-eye distance for each matching algorithm when the threshold is fixed. The figure demonstrates the behavior of a system that applies the same decision threshold to all comparisons regardless of inter-eye distance. In the figure, all algorithms show the same trend: higher FNMR and lower FMR for smaller inter-eye distances. The fact that the FMR never increases when the inter-eye distance is reduced is desirable. It means that any verification system operating at a fixed threshold and employing one of these algorithms would NOT be susceptible to accepting false claims of identity when comparing face images that have low pixel resolutions.

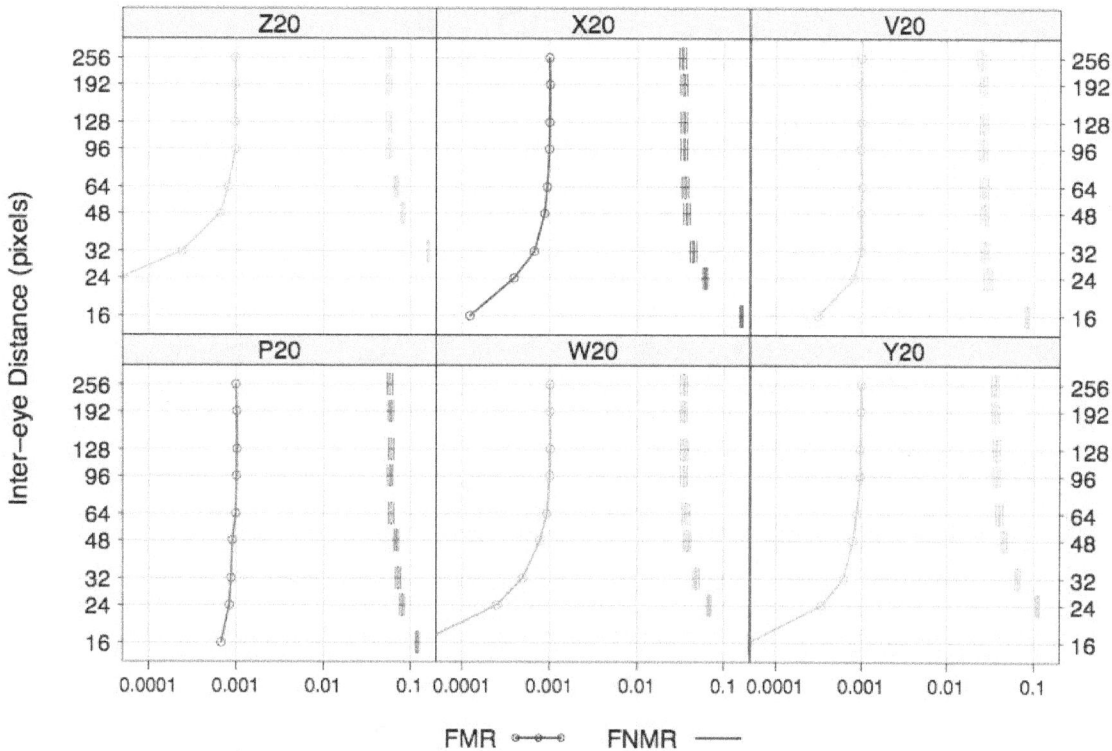

Figure 5. FNMR (left) and FMR (right) as a function of the inter-eye distance when the decision threshold is fixed at an FMR of 0.001 on uncompressed images.

Recommendations and Conclusions:

1) Images should be tokenized to no less than 96 pixels between the eyes to ensure optimal recognition accuracy. This is stricter than the ISO/IEC 19794-5 requirement of 60.

2) Inter-eye distances above 96 pixels provide no perceivable benefit in terms of recognition accuracy.

3) For some matchers recognition accuracy deteriorates when the inter-eye distance drops below 96 pixels, although one of the matchers is capable of effectively comparing enrollment images with inter-eye distances as low as 24 pixels.

4) Lower inter-eye distances tend to correspond to higher false non-match rates and lower false match rates. Reducing the inter-eye distance of token images never increases the false match rate, which is desirable to prevent a system from accepting poor quality samples.

6.2. JPEG Compression

Purpose: To determine the effect of JPEG compression on recognition accuracy.

Since the current matching algorithms benefit little from inter-eye distances above 96 pixels, it makes sense to scale the image resolution down such that the inter-eye distance is 96 pixels before applying JPEG compression. Figure 6 plots FNMR (at FMR=0.001) as a function of file size for all 6 algorithms. The degree to which accuracy depends on the file size varies for each algorithm. Some algorithms (P20 and V20) can tolerate high amounts of compression (down to 8000 bytes) with little loss in accuracy, while other algorithms (Z20 and Y20) begin to show a drop in accuracy a bit earlier, at 16000 bytes.

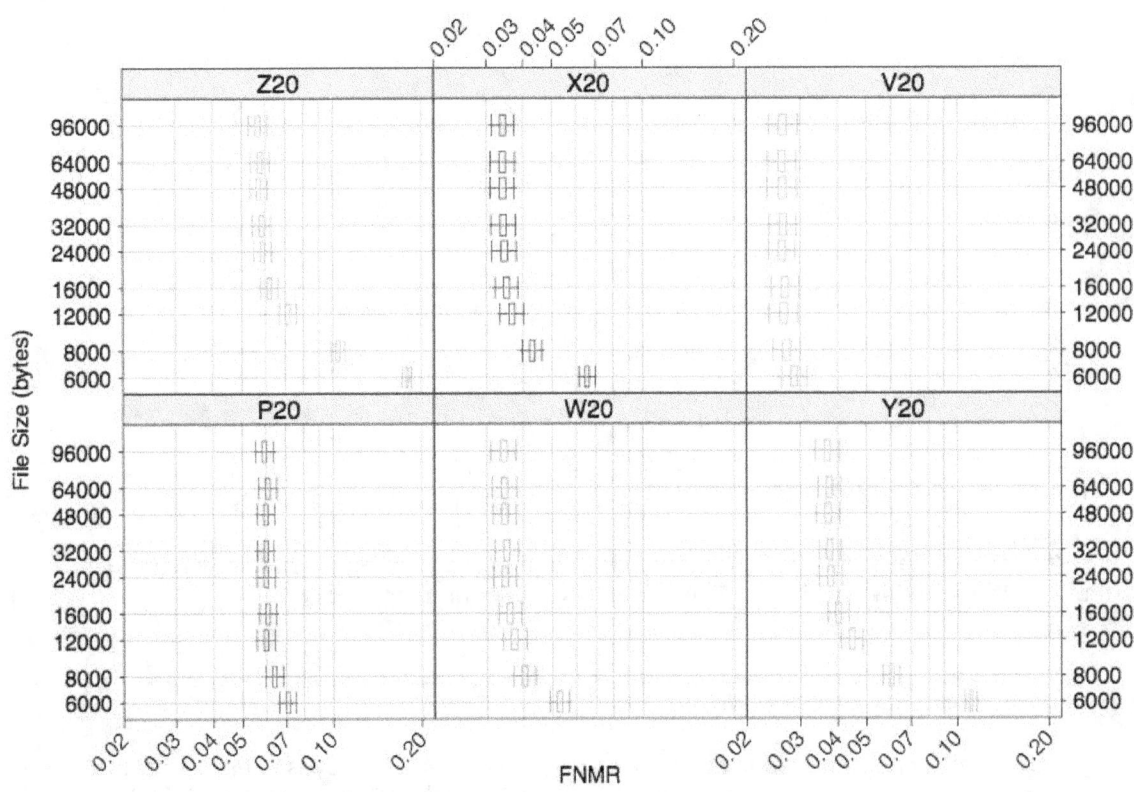

Figure 6. FNMR (at FMR=0.001) as a function of file size when enrollment images are JPEG compressed. The inter-eye distance of the enrollment images was fixed at 96 pixels.

Figure 7 shows the visual effects of compressing a token image to various file sizes. Although some algorithms experience a minor drop in accuracy around 16000 bytes, compression artifacts are typically not visibly apparent until the images are compressed to much smaller sizes. "Blocking" artifacts are not obvious in the presented image until the file size is reduced to 8000 bytes, although the skin texture appears slightly defocused at 12000 bytes. At 6000 bytes, blocking is plainly apparent and significant noise is introduced, especially around areas of sharp contrast.

| Uncompressed | 12000 bytes | 8000 bytes | 6000 bytes |

Figure 7. A tokenized face image from MEDS-I compressed to various sizes with JPEG. The inter-eye distance was adjusted to 96 pixels. (Artifacts may not present themselves well on paper printouts).

As was done in Section 6.1, we explore the effect of compression when the decision threshold is fixed across all levels of compression.. Figure 8 plots FMR and FNMR as a function of file size when enrollment images are JPEG compressed to the indicated file size. Note that by comparison, the box plots Figure 6 had the decision threshold adjusted at each inter-eye distance to elicit an FMR of 0.001. The figure highlights how a system would behave if the same decision threshold were applied to all comparisons, regardless of compression amount. For all algorithms, greater amounts of compression typically correspond to higher false non-match rates and lower false match rates. The FMR never increases in response to greater amounts of compression. Below 4000, JPEG is incapable of producing enrollment images of the required size for the majority of the images. A solution would be to reduce the inter-eye distance and then apply JPEG compression (which will be addressed later in the section). This would likely further increase the false non-match rate and possibly reduce the false match rate.

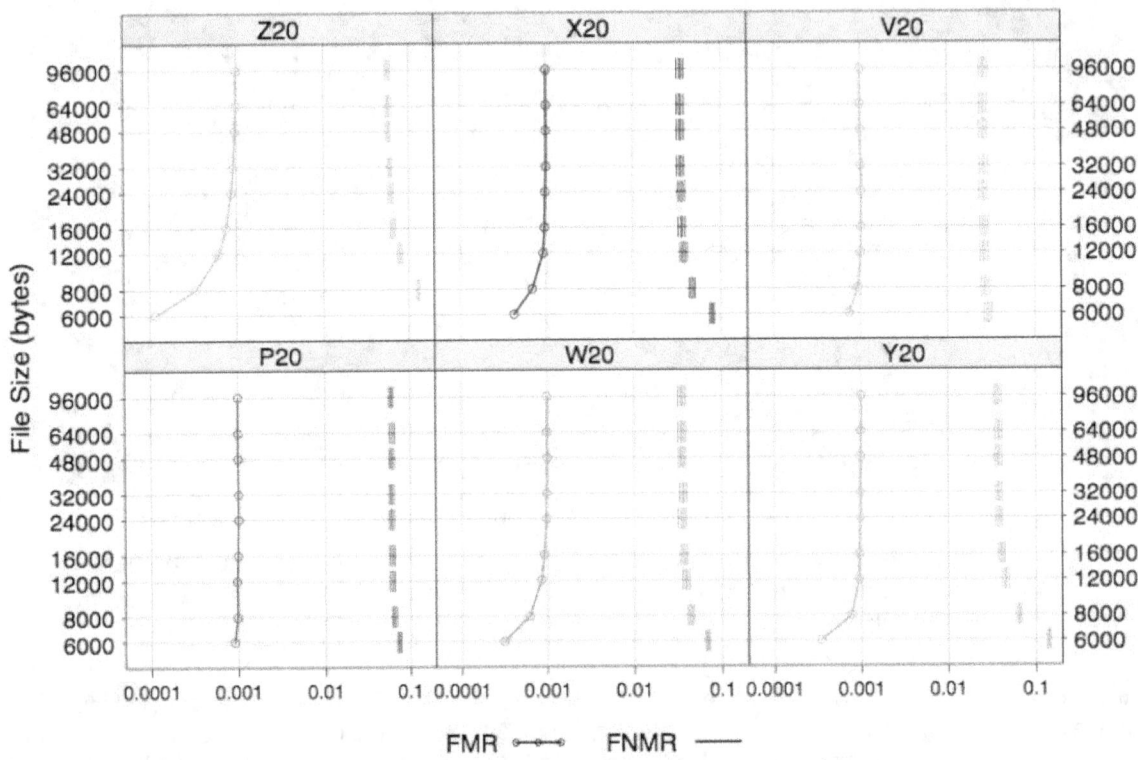

Figure 8. FMR (left) and FNMR (right) as a function of file size when enrollment images are JPEG compressed. The inter-eye distance was fixed at 96, and the threshold was set to produce an FMR=0.001 on uncompressed images.

JPEG is limited with respect to the minimum size at which it can compress images. Table 2 shows the failure to compress rates (FTC) for JPEG images at various file sizes and inter-eye distances. A failure to compress occurs when JPEG cannot reduce the size of the file to the given target, even at quality 0. JPEG has more difficulty compressing images when the inter-eye distance is large. For example, JPEG can only compress tokenized Sandia images to 6000 bytes when the inter-eye distance is 96 pixels or fewer, but at 2000 bytes, the cut-off is at 48 pixels. In most cases the cut-off point is quite sharply defined. For example, at 2000 bytes, all face images with inter-eye distances of 48 or fewer pixels were successfully compressed while all images with inter-eye distances above 48 pixels failed to compress.

| | | File Size (bytes) | | | | | | | | | | | |
		2000	3000	4000	6000	8000	12000	16000	24000	32000	48000	64000	96000
Inter-eye Distance (pixels)	16	0.00	0.00	0.00	0.00	0.00	0.00	0.00	0.00	0.00	0.00	0.00	0.00
	24	0.00	0.00	0.00	0.00	0.00	0.00	0.00	0.00	0.00	0.00	0.00	0.00
	32	0.00	0.00	0.00	0.00	0.00	0.00	0.00	0.00	0.00	0.00	0.00	0.00
	48	0.00	0.00	0.00	0.00	0.00	0.00	0.00	0.00	0.00	0.00	0.00	0.00
	64	1.00	0.00	0.00	0.00	0.00	0.00	0.00	0.00	0.00	0.00	0.00	0.00
	96	1.00	1.00	0.76	0.00	0.00	0.00	0.00	0.00	0.00	0.00	0.00	0.00
	128	1.00	1.00	1.00	1.00	0.00	0.00	0.00	0.00	0.00	0.00	0.00	0.00
	192	1.00	1.00	1.00	1.00	1.00	1.00	0.00	0.00	0.00	0.00	0.00	0.00

| 256 | 1.00 | 1.00 | 1.00 | 1.00 | 1.00 | 1.00 | 1.00 | 0.32 | 0.00 | 0.00 | 0.00 | 0.00 |

Table 2. Failure to Compress Rates on tokenized Sandia images for various file sizes and inter-eye distances. A value of 1.00 indicates no images with the given inter-eye distance could be compressed to the specified file size.

Recommendations and Conclusions:

1) To maintain optimal recognition accuracy, token face images with an inter-eye distance of 96 pixels should be JPEG compressed to no fewer than 24000 bytes.

2) Some algorithms are much better at matching compressed JPEG images than others. One algorithm is capable of matching enrollment images compressed to 6000 bytes without a significant loss in accuracy.

3) Greater amounts of JPEG compression tend to correspond to higher false non-match rates and lower false match rates. Increasing the amount of JPEG compression never increases the false match rate, which is desirable to prevent the system from falsely accepting poor quality samples.

4) Token face images with smaller inter-eye distances can be compressed to smaller file sizes. At 12000 bytes, JPEG allows images to have inter-eye distances of 128 or fewer pixels. This does not necessarily mean that face images will match best at this inter-eye distance.

6.3.   JPEG Compression with Inter-eye Distance Reduction

Purpose: To find the best way to combine inter-eye distance reduction with JPEG compression such that recognition accuracy is minimally affected.

JPEG compression can be applied in tandem with inter-eye distance reduction. Figure 9 shows matching accuracy as a function of both. Enrollment images were down-sampled during tokenization to the specified inter-eye distance and subsequently compressed using JPEG to the specified file size. The FNMR (at FMR=0.001) is indicated by the color of each cell. Cells are left white if any of the enrollment images having the given inter-eye distance could not be compressed to the target file size, even at a JPEG quality level of 0 (see Section 6.3 on failure to compress).

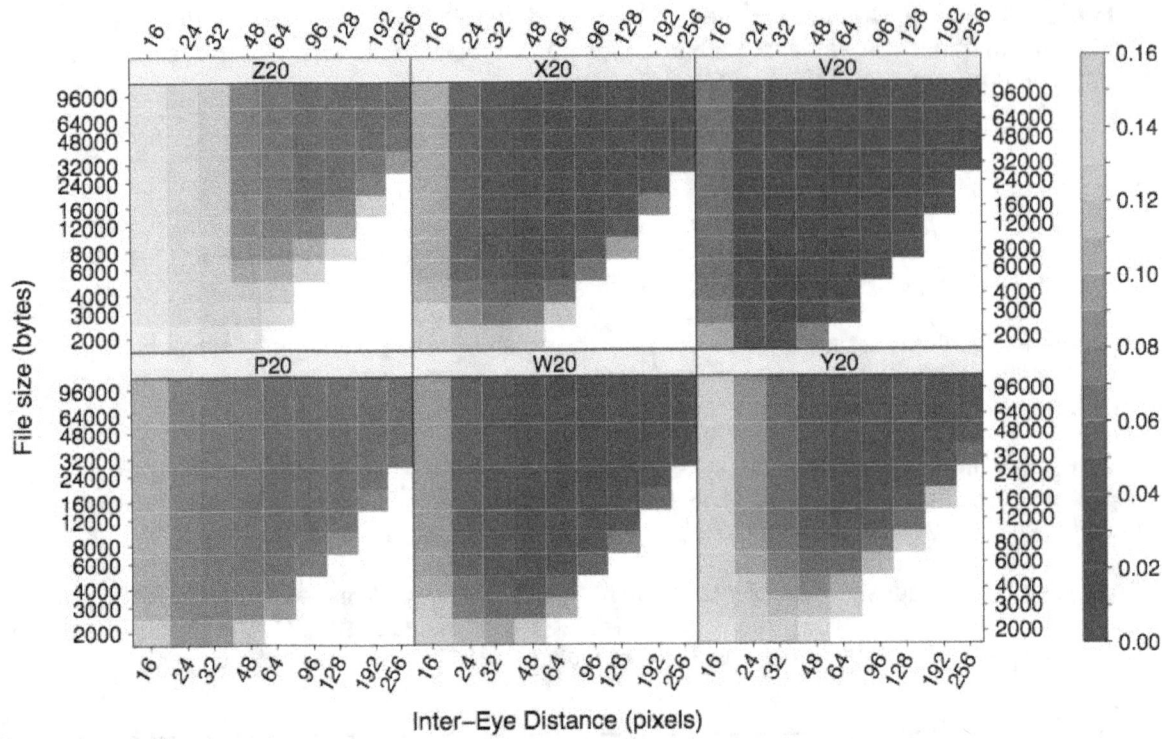

Figure 9. FNMR (indicated by color) at FMR=0.001 as a function of JPEG compression (vertical axis) and inter-eye distance (horizontal axis). Enrollment images were down-sampled to the specified inter-eye distance and subsequently compressed to the specified file size.

The figure reveals that for any particular file size, there is typically an ideal range of inter-eye distances that produce the lowest error. This can be seen by looking at any horizontal slice of blocks for any of the algorithms and noticing that in most cases the FNMR is higher at the extreme left and right ends. The ideal range tends to shift toward lower inter-eye distances as the target file size reduces. This indicates that there is often a benefit to reducing the inter-eye distance prior to compressing the images with JPEG. For clarity, this is highlighted more precisely in Figure 10. The figure shows FNMR as a function of the inter-eye distance at several targeted file sizes for X20. Each curve in the figure corresponds to a horizontal slice of blocks in Figure 9. The curves for smaller target file sizes have local minima translated farther to the left, again demonstrating the benefit to reducing the inter-eye distance prior to compressing the images with JPEG. The dips tend to be much more pronounced for smaller target file sizes, revealing that matching accuracy is more sensitive to the inter-eye distance when the file size is small (at least for X20).

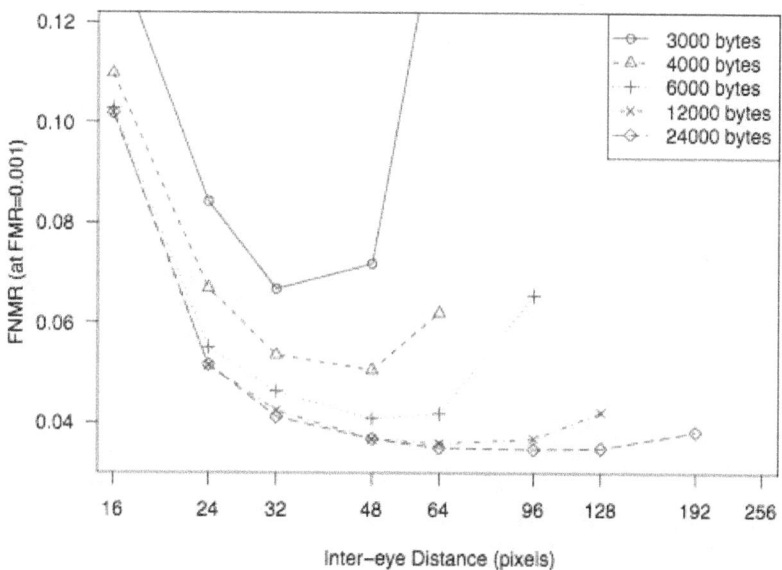

Figure 10. FNMR (at FMR=0.001) as a function of inter-eye distance for various targeted file sizes when enrollment images are JPEG compressed. Performance is shown for X20.

The relationship between file size and ideal inter-eye distance appears to be approximately linear in the log space. If we regard the target file size as the independent variable (x) and the ideal inter-eye distance as the dependent variable (y), then the relationship is

$$\log(y) = a\log(x) + b \qquad (1)$$

which is equivalent to

$$y = a'x^{b'} \qquad (2)$$

where a' and b' are unknown parameters. Equation (2) was used to construct a model that, when fitted, allows us to predict the optimal inter-eye distance for a given target file size. The first step in constructing the model was to compute the log of the mean FNMR among all six algorithms for each combination of inter-eye distance and target file size. These values can be used to create a discrete surface where the log of the mean FNMR is indicated by the z-coordinate (somewhat similar to the heatmaps presented in Figure 9, where FNMR is indicated by color rather than z-coordinate). The surface was then fit with two-dimensional splines to allow interpolation at arbitrary file sizes and inter-eye distances. The optimization step used the Nelder-Mead method [25] of minimizing a cost function given a' and b' as the varying parameters. The cost function was the line integral of equation (2) over the fitted surface. The reason integration was performed over the log of the mean FNMR rather than the mean FNMR is because the former assigns more weight to areas of low error, which are of greater operationally relevancy.

The results of fitting the model are presented in Figure 11. The colors on the surface are a rough indicator of the log of the mean FNMR (where red corresponds to lower error) and the best-fit line is shown in light blue. The table on the right shows the predicted ideal inter-eye distance for various targeted file sizes. The derived values for the unknown parameters are $a' = 0.464$ and $b' = 0.546$ (when the inter-eye distance is in pixels, and the target file size is in bytes). The fitted values of the model provide a good rule of thumb that holds fairly closely for each of the algorithms used in this study. Note that since most algorithms experience no benefit for inter-eye distances above 96 pixels, there should be no reason to reduce the inter-eye distance to values above this value. Therefore, when an image must be compressed with JPEG, we suggest the inter-eye distance be reduced according to

$$y = \min\left\{0.464x^{0.546}, \ 96\right\} \tag{3}$$

where, to re-iterate, x is the targeted file size in bytes, and y is the model's prediction of the ideal inter-eye distance, in pixels. If the inter-eye distance is already smaller than the predicted value, no up-scaling should be performed. Note that while the model predicts the ideal inter-eye distance, some algorithms are less sensitive to variations in the inter-eye distance than others. For example, the uniformity of the colors across the cells for V20 in Figure 9 suggests that the ideal inter-eye distance for this algorithm is not unique and typically covers a wide range of values.

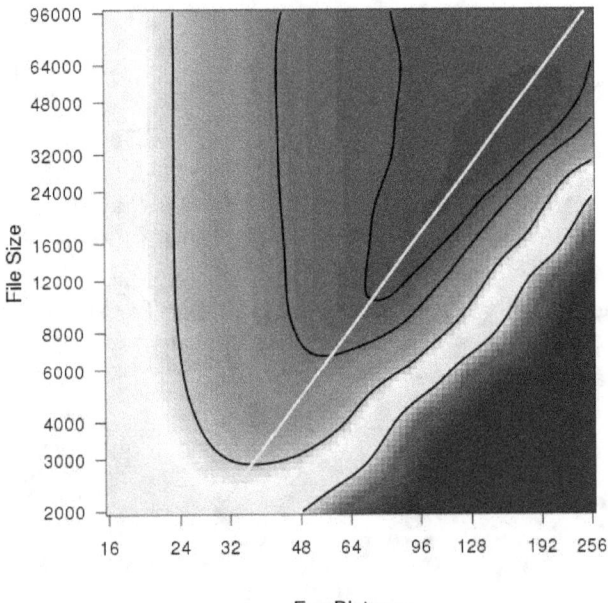

File Size (bytes)	Predicted Ideal Inter-eye Distance (pixels)
2000	29.4
3000	36.7
4000	43.0
6000	53.6
8000	62.7
12000	78.3
16000	91.6
24000	114.3

Eye Distance

Figure 11 Results of fitting the model. At left, colors correspond to mean FNMR among all 6 algorithms (where red indicates lower error) according to a spline fit of the data. The best-fit line is shown in light blue. The table at right shows predictions of the optimal inter-eye distance at various file sizes.

Recommendations and Conclusions:

1) When at least 24000 bytes are available for storing each enrollment image, the inter-eye distance should be reduced to 96 pixels to ensure that JPEG compression does not adversely affect recognition accuracy.

2) When fewer than 24000 bytes per image are available, the inter-eye distance should be reduced according to equation (3) to minimize the expected impact of JPEG compression on recognition accuracy.

3) Some algorithms are much less sensitive to variations in the inter-eye distance than others when images are compressed with JPEG. Nevertheless, the inter-eye distance should still be adjusted

according to equation (3) to maintain inter-operability and to ensure that the token images will match well across vendors.

4) The most accurate algorithm is capable of matching enrollment images compressed to 4000 bytes without a significant loss in accuracy, but it requires a considerable reduction of the inter-eye distance that would renders such images unsuitable for human analysis.

6.4. JPEG2000 Compression

Purpose: To determine the effect of JPEG2000 compression on matching accuracy.

This section performs a similar analysis to Section 6.2 but for JPEG2000 compression. Figure 12 plots FNMR (at FMR=0.001) as a function of file size when images are JPEG2000 compressed. As in Section 6.2, the inter-eye distance of the compressed images was fixed at 96 pixels. The dependency of matching accuracy on the amount of compression varies for the different algorithms. Some (P20 and V20) can tolerate high amounts of compression (down to 12000 bytes) while experiencing only small increases in FNMR. Even at 8000 bytes FNMR is only slightly raised for these two algorithms. Other algorithms (Z20, X20, and Y20) show an increasing trend in FNMR much earlier. Note that although P20 demonstrates greater resilience to JPEG2000 compression, its overall performance still often lags behind many of the other algorithms. For example, X20 is less tolerant of JPEG2000 compression, but still outperforms P20 at file sizes greater than 3000 bytes.

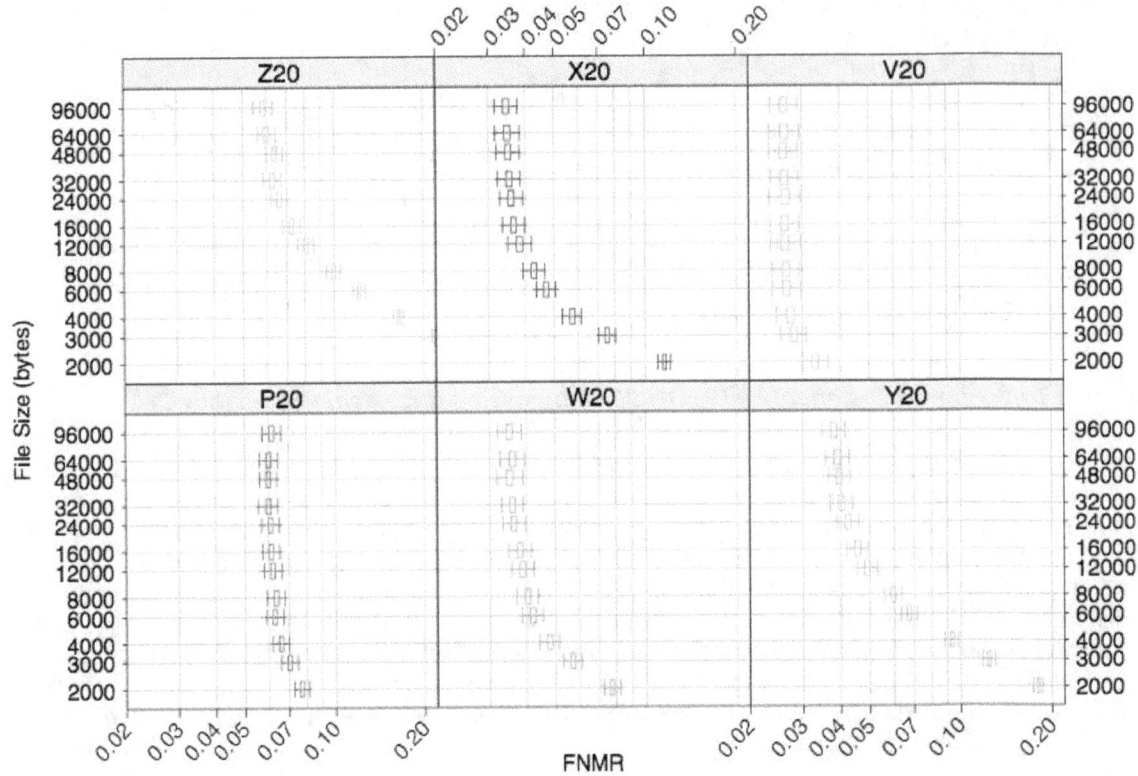

Figure 12. FNMR (at FMR=0.001) as a function of file size when enrollment images are JPEG2000 compressed. The inter-eye distance of enrollment images was fixed at 96 pixels.

Figure 13 demonstrates the visible effects of JPEG2000 compression on a token face image. Although difficult to see, the skin texture of the individual is quite significantly smoothed at 6000 bytes. The smoothing is more apparent at smaller file sizes and at 2000 bytes the edge of the individual's cheek is blurry and poorly defined. The algorithms that show the least tolerance for JPEG2000 compression may rely more heavily on the high frequency information in the images (e.g. the skin texture), which is preferentially discarded by JPEG2000.

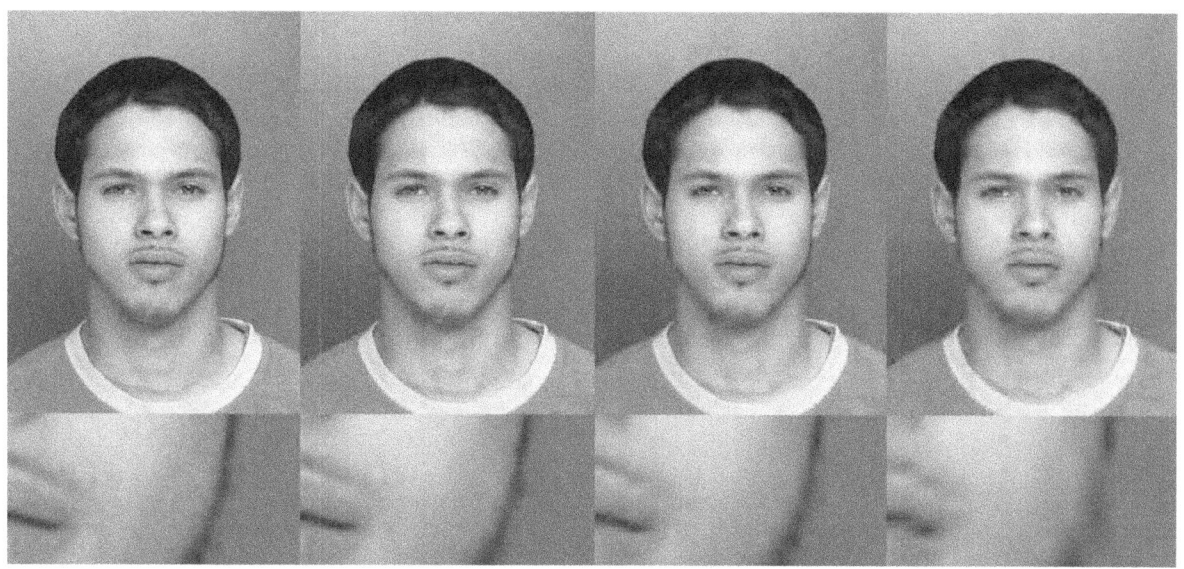

| Uncompressed | 6000 bytes | 3000 bytes | 2000 bytes |

Figure 13. Example of a token face image compressed at various sizes using JPEG2000. The image is from MEDS-I and the inter-eye distance is fixed at 96 pixels.

Figure 14 plots both FMR and FNMR as a function of file size when enrollment images are JPEG2000 compressed to the indicated file size. Note that by comparison, the box plots in Figure 13 had the threshold adjusted at each inter-eye distance to elicit an FMR of 0.001. In the current figure, the threshold was fixed across all box plots. The figure is meant to highlight the behavior of a system that applies the same decision threshold to all comparisons, regardless of the amount of compression. For all algorithms, greater amounts of compression typically correspond to higher false non-match rates and lower false match rates. The false match rate never increases in respond to greater amounts of compression. This is a desirable property since it means the algorithms are not susceptible to spoofing if intentionally presented with a severely compressed image.

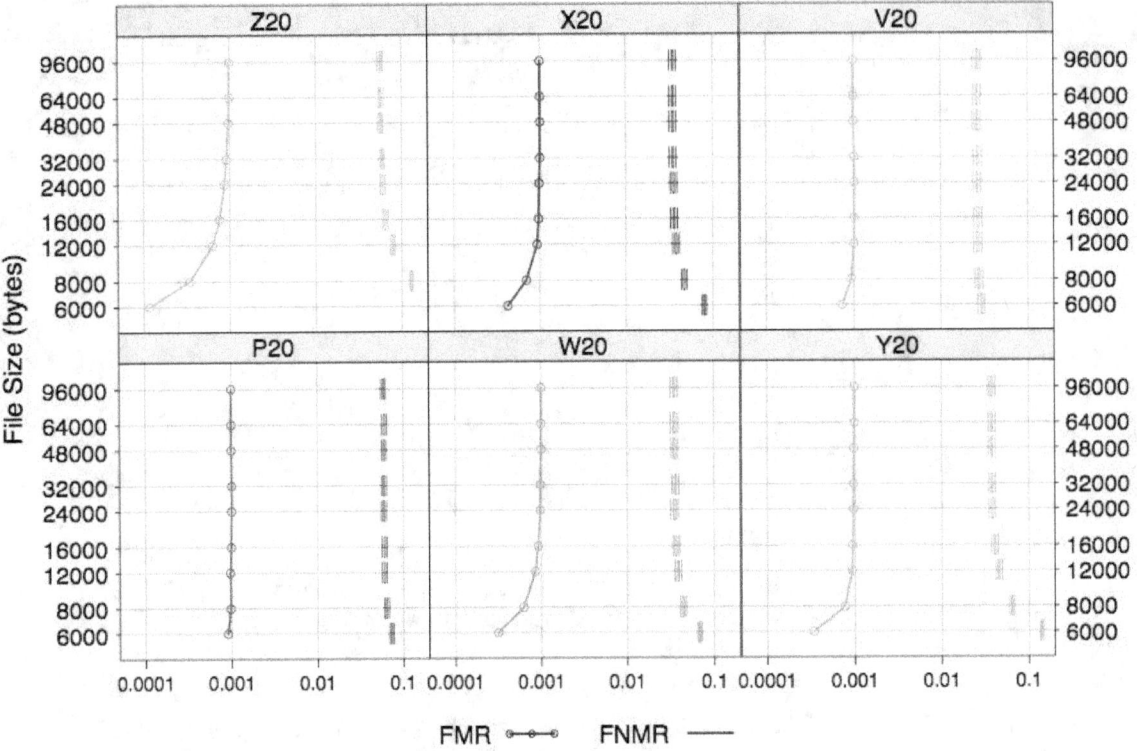

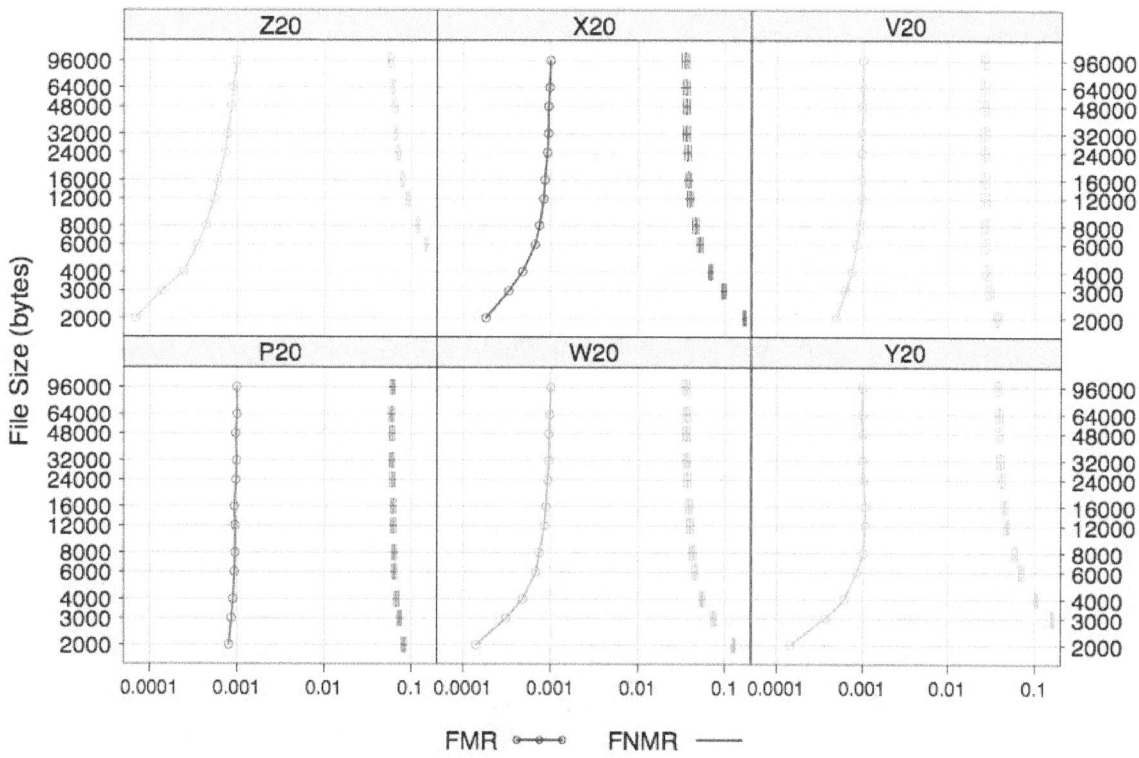

Figure 14 FNMR (left) and FMR (right) as a function of file size when images are JPEG2000 compressed. The inter-eye distance of enrollment images is fixed at 96, and the threshold is set to elicit an FMR of 0.001 on uncompressed face images.

Recommendations and Conclusions:

1) Some algorithms are much better at matching compressed JPEG2000 images than others. Oen algorithm is capable of handling enrollment images compressed to as little as 3000 bytes without a significant loss in accuracy.

2) Some algorithms (Y20, Z20) experience a drop in matching accuracy even when the enrollment images are JPEG2000 compressed to large file sizes (24000 bytes). This contraindicates the use of JPEG2000 when more than 16000 bytes are available for storing the image.

3) Greater amounts of JPEG2000 compression tend to correspond to higher false non-match rates and lower false match rates. Increasing the amount of JPEG2000 compression never increases the false match rate, which is desirable to prevent spoofing.

6.5. JPEG2000 Compression with Inter-eye Distance Reduction

Purpose: To determine if there is an accuracy benefit to reducing the inter-eye distance prior to applying JPEG2000 compression.

JPEG2000 compression can be applied in tandem with inter-eye distance reduction, similar to what was done for JPEG in Section 6.3. Figure 15 shows matching accuracy as a function of both inter-eye distance and JPEG2000 compression. Enrollment images were down-sampled during the tokenization step to the specified inter-eye distance and subsequently compressed using JPEG2000 to the specified file size. The color in each cell indicates the FNMR (at FMR=0.001) for the given combination of inter-eye distance and target file size. The figure reveals a significant difference in the way that JPEG and JPEG2000 compression affect recognition accuracy. Unlike JPEG (see Section 6.3), JPEG2000 is never detrimentally affected by large inter-eye distances. This can be seen by looking at any horizontal slice of blocks for any of the algorithms and noticing that the right-most block (corresponding to the largest inter-eye distance) always has an FNMR at least as low as any of the other blocks. This point is highlighted more precisely in Figure 16, which shows FNMR as a function of the inter-eye distance at several targeted file sizes. Unlike JPEG, no local minima are present, again emphasizing that there is never a performance benefit to down-sampling the pixel resolution before applying JPEG2000 compression. The reason for this is likely due to the similar way in which pixel resolution down-sampling and JPEG2000 compression both selectively discard the higher frequency information in an image, albeit by different methods.

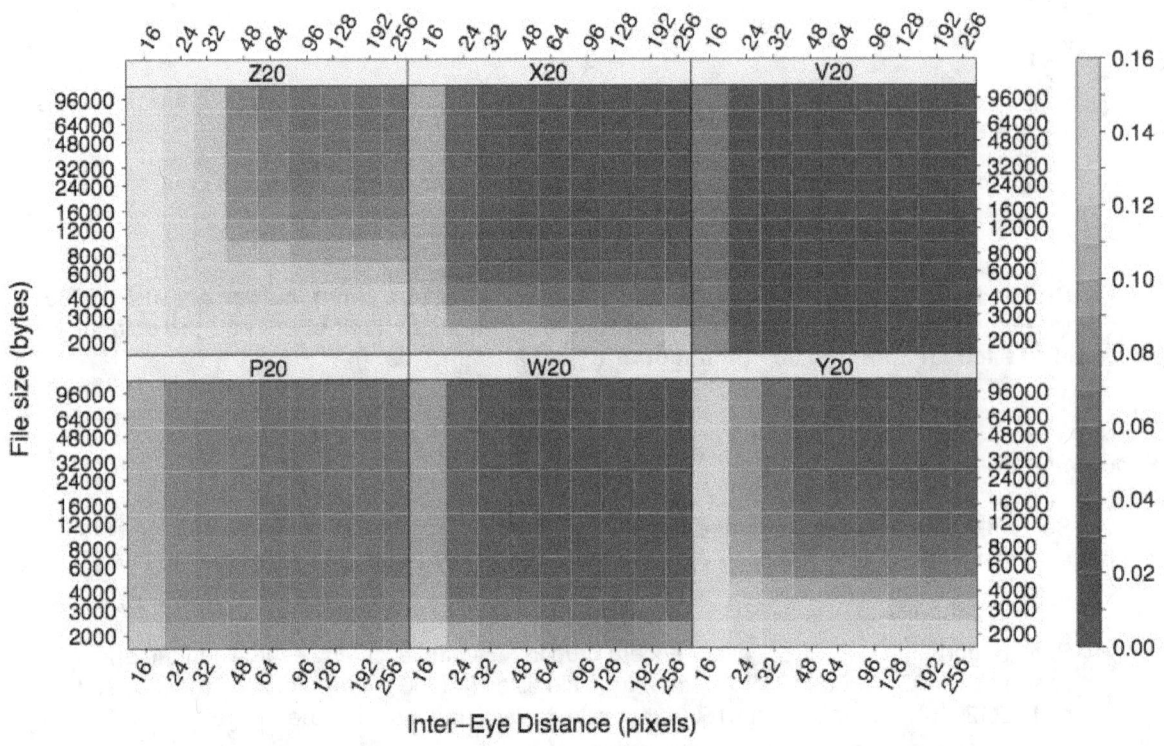

Figure 15. FNMR (indicated by cell color) at FMR=0.001 as a function of JPEG2000 compression (vertical axis) and inter-eye distance (horizontal axis). Enrollment images were down-sampled to the specified inter-eye distance and then compressed to the specified file size using JPEG2000.

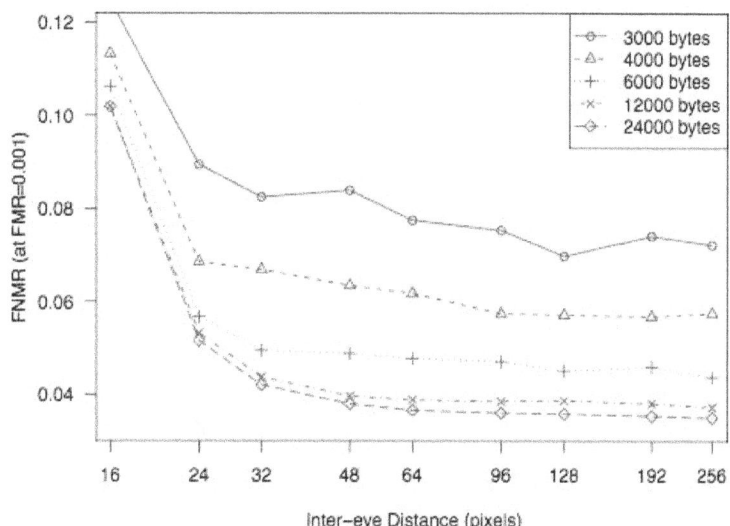

Figure 16. FNMR (at FMR=0.001) as a function of inter-eye distance for various targeted file sizes when JPEG2000 compression is used. Performance is shown for X20.

Recommendations and Conclusions:

1) The most accurate algorithm is capable of matching enrollment images compressed to 3000 bytes almost as well as uncompressed images. Although such images are suitable for automated verification, the visible artifacts introduced by severe compression render them unsuitable for human analysis.

2) The inter-eye distance of face images should not be reduced if the images are JPEG2000 compressed. Face images with large inter-eye distances always match at least as well as corresponding images stored at lower inter-eye distances.

6.6. *JPEG vs. JPEG2000 Compression*

Purpose: To 1) compare the performance of JPEG and JPEG2000 compression in terms of matching accuracy, and 2) to identify which method of compression should be used under which circumstances.

The generally held belief is that JPEG2000 is better at compressing images than traditional JPEG. This is a reasonable assumption considering JPEG2000 was developed to supersede JPEG and uses newer wavelet technology. JPEG2000 also demonstrated itself far superior at compressing standard iris images [20] for matching purposes. However, the results presented in this study indicate that there are some circumstances (specifically, when the file size is large) when compressing with traditional JPEG is better than compressing with JPEG2000.

Figure 17 provides a direct comparison of JPEG and JPEG2000 compression by plotting the performance of both as a function of file size. The figure reveals that for four of the algorithms (Z20, X20, W20, Y20), there is a crossover point at which JPEG2000 achieves lower error rates at smaller file sizes, and JPEG achieves lower error rates at larger file sizes. The locations of the crossover points are likely to vary depending on the inter-eye distance. For the remaining two algorithms, JPEG2000 performs at least as well as JPEG. The benefit to using JPEG is often small if present, constituting only a 0.01 difference in FNMR or less. At small file sizes (< 8000 bytes), JPEG experiences catastrophic failure while JPEG2000 is still capable of maintaining reasonable error rates.

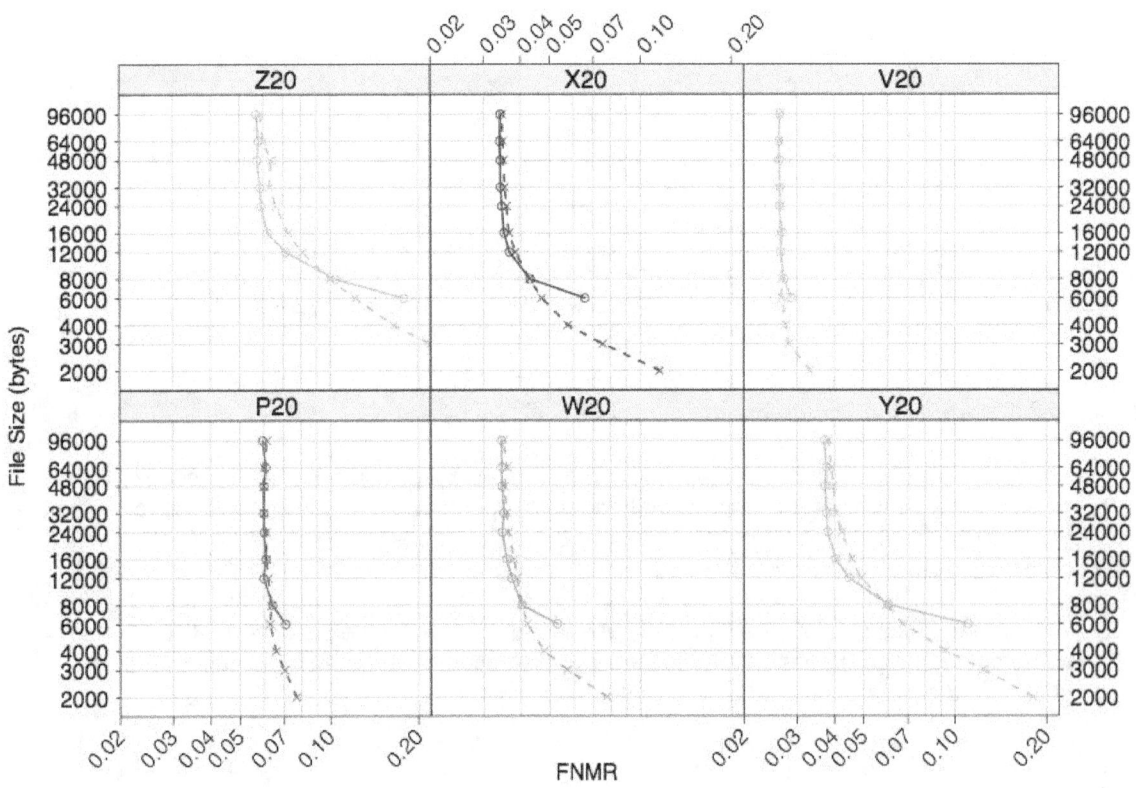

Figure 17. FNMR (at FMR=0.001) as a function of file size for JPEG (solid line) and JPEG2000 (dotted line) when the inter-eye distance is fixed at 96 pixels.

Figure 18 plots the average PSNR as a function of file size for JPEG and JPEG2000. By this measure, JPEG2000 consistently outperforms JPEG over the entire range of file sizes. JPEG2000 achieves lossless compression at 96000 bytes on some images, so the point cannot be plotted. JPEG appears to asymptote to a PSNR around 38 as the file size increases, most likely as a result of its lossy method of color quantization, which prevents lossless compression from ever being achieved. Strictly according to the PSNR, JPEG2000's method of compression seems to provide greater fidelity to the original image than traditional JPEG. This contrasts with the results from Figure 17, which shows JPEG sometimes outperforms JPEG2000 in terms of recognition accuracy. Regardless of whether the differences in accuracy are statistically significant, the authors conclude that while PSNR provides a good general measure of the degree of image corruption, it is not a strong predictor of recognition accuracy because it does not account for the specific ways in which algorithms extract matchable features from face images.

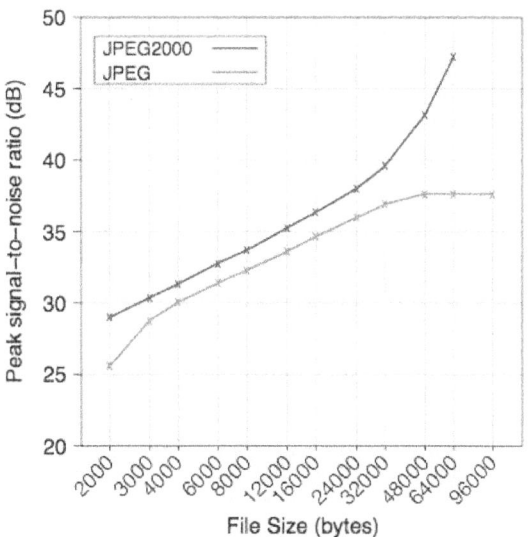

Figure 18. Average Peak signal-to-noise ratio (PSNR) as a function of file size for JPEG and JPEG2000. Enrollment images were scaled to an inter-eye distance of 48 pixels. JPEG2000 outperforms JPEG.

Recommendations and Conclusions:

1) At larger file sizes (>16000 bytes), JPEG often offers a small performance benefit over JPEG2000. For larger file sizes (>24000 bytes) traditional JPEG should be used.

2) At very small file sizes (< 8000 bytes) JPEG2000 is the better option since it achieves far lower error rates and does not require a reduction of the inter-eye distance to avoid high error rates (see Section 6.2).

3) PSNR is not a strong predictor of how compression affects matching accuracy and should not be used for that purpose.

6.7. JPEG Grayscale Compression

Purpose: To determine the performance benefits to storing face images as grayscale JPEGs.

Converting an image from color to grayscale significantly reduces its storage requirement, and most matching algorithms are capable of comparing grayscale images as well as color. Figure 19 plots FNMR as a function of file size when enrollment images are JPEG compressed as either grayscale or color images. At larger file sizes (>16000 bytes) there is no benefit to storing an image in grayscale (although there is no harm either). However, at smaller file sizes (<8000 bytes) all algorithms perform better when comparing grayscale enrollment images, and the difference becomes more pronounced at smaller file sizes.

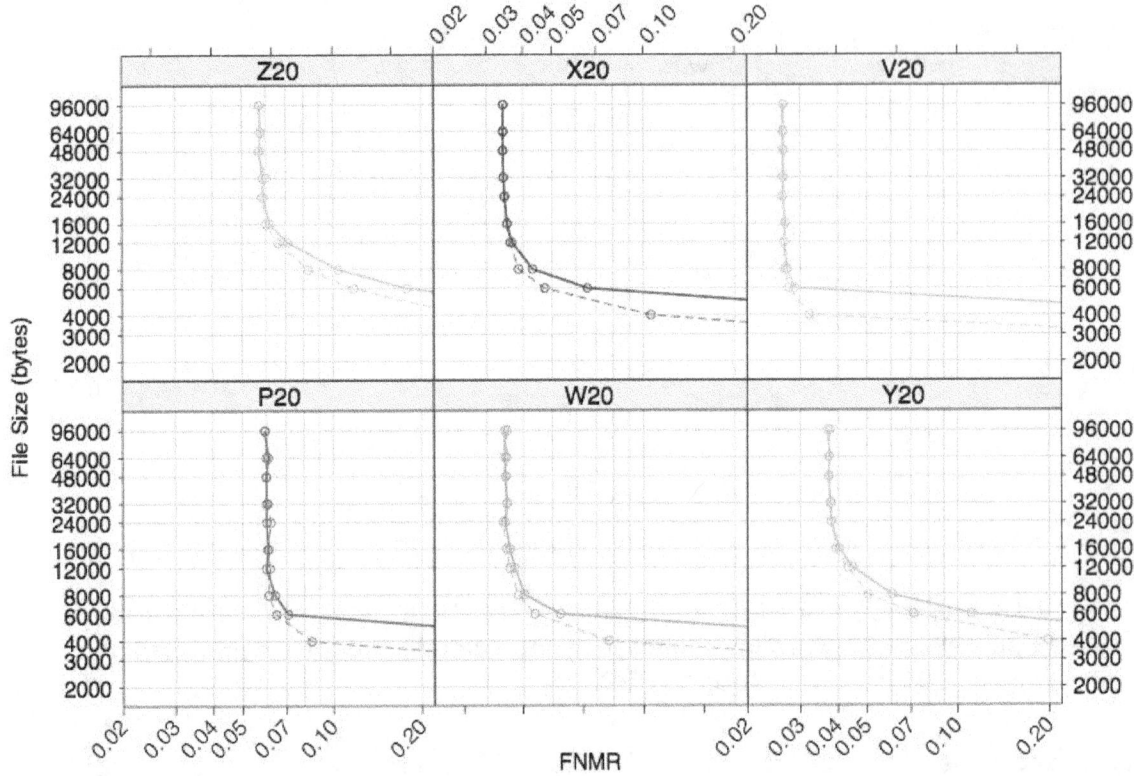

Figure 19. FNMR (at FMR=0.001) as a function of file size when enrollment images are JPEG compressed in color (solid line) and grayscale (dotted line). The inter-eye distance for enrollment images was fixed at 96 pixels.

Figure 20 shows FNMR as a function of file size for the best performing algorithm when the inter-eye distance of enrollment images is reduced to 32 pixels. Even at 2000 bytes the FNMR is only slightly raised over what is seen at larger inter-eye distances and file sizes. Although this demonstrates that V20 is capable of comparing tokenized images compressed to as little as 2000 bytes, the small inter-eye distance and high compression ratio renders such images unsuitable for human inspection.

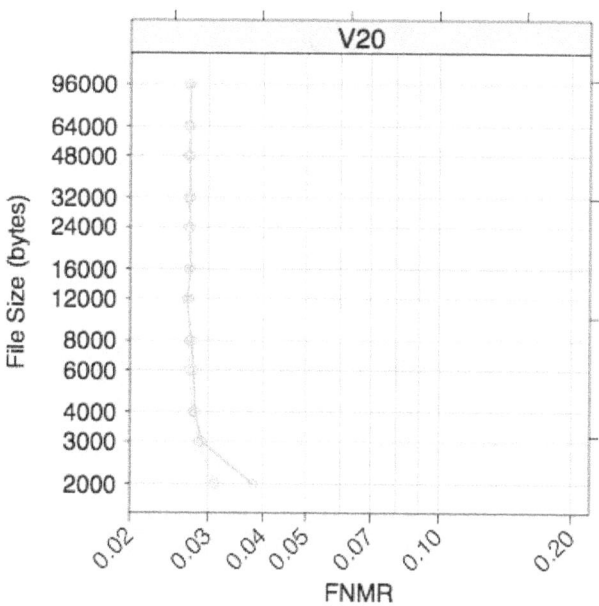

Figure 20. FNMR (at FMR=0.001) as a function of file size for V20 when enrollment images are stored in color (solid line) and grayscale (dotted line). The inter-eye distance was set at 32 pixels.

Recommendations:

1) Converting images to grayscale never detrimentally affects recognition accuracy for any of the algorithms. At large file sizes (>16000 bytes), there is never an accuracy benefit to converting images to grayscale. At smaller file sizes, there is often a performance benefit.

2) One of the more accurate algorithms is capable of effectively comparing against enrollment images compressed to as little as 2000 bytes. Although suitable for verification purposes, such images would not be suitable for human analysis.

6.8. JPEG2000 Grayscale Compression

Purpose: To determine whether there is a performance benefit to storing JPEG2000 face images in grayscale.

JPEG2000 also supports a grayscale storage format. Figure 21 plots FNMR as a function of file size when enrollment images are stored as either grayscale or color images. The figure indicates that storing images in JPEG2000 grayscale never offers a substantial performance benefit over corresponding color images, although it is never harmful either. For two algorithms (Z20 and Y20) there is a small reduction in FNMR for grayscale images that is more noticeable at smaller file sizes. However, in both cases the difference may not be statistically significant.

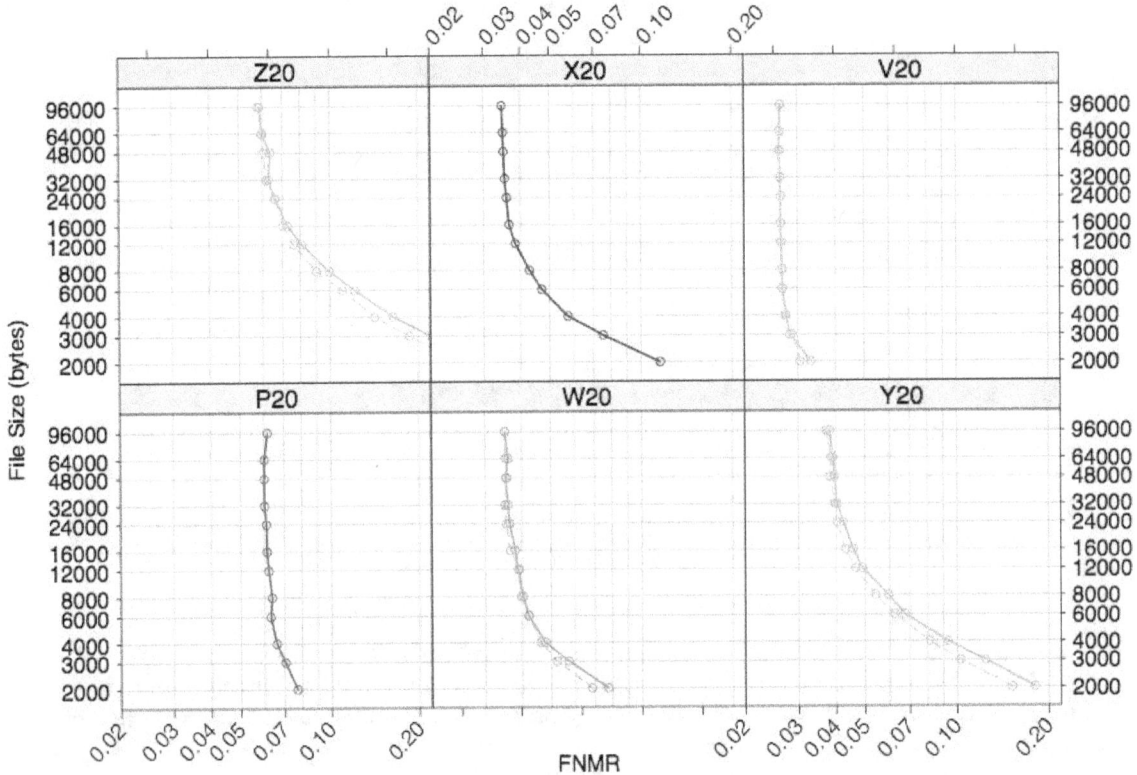

Figure 21 FNMR (at FMR=0.001) as a function of file size when enrollment images are JPEG2000 compressed in color (solid line) and grayscale (dotted line). The inter-eye distance for enrollment images was fixed at 96 pixels.

Conclusions:

Empirical results indicate that storing compressed JPEG2000 images in grayscale never offers a significant accuracy benefit over storing them in color. The reason for this is unclear.

7.   References

[1]   ISO/IEC 19794-5 Information Technology – Biometric Data Interchange Formats – Part 5: Face Image Data. JTC 1/SC 37, international standard edition, 2005. http:/isotc.iso.org/isotcportal. Accessed March 15, 2011.

[2]   Federal Information Processing Standards 201-1: Personal Identity Verification (PIV) of Federal Employees and Contractors. NIST. http://csrc.nist.gov/publications/PubsFIPS.html. Accessed March 15, 2011.

[3]   ANSI/NIST ITL 2007: Data Format for the Interchange of Fingerprint, Facial & Other Biometric Information. NIST Special Publication 500-271, April, 2007.

[4]   P. Grother, G. W. Quinn, and J. Phillips. Report on the Evaluation of 2D Still-Image Face Recognition Algorithms. Technical Report. National Institute of Standards and Technology, June 2010. Published as NIST Interagency Report 7709.

[5]   J. Phillips, T. Scruggs, A. O'Toole, P. Flynn, K. Bowyer, C. Schott, and M. Sharpe. FRVT 2006 and ICE 2006 Large-Scale Results. Technical Report. National Institute of Standards and Technology, March 2007. Published as NIST Interagency Report 7408.

[6]   J. Phillips, P. Grother, R. Michaels, D. Blackburn, E. Tabassi, M. Bone. Face Recognition Vendor Test 2002. Technical Report. National Institute of Standards and Technology, March 2003. Published as NIST Interagency Report 6965.

[7]   K. Delac, M. Grgic, and S. Grgic. Effects of JPEG and JPEG2000 Compression on Face Recognition. In *Proceedings of ICAPR 2005, LLNCS 3687.* pages 136-145, 2005.

[8]   *The FERET Database.* NIST, 2003. Web. February, 2011. http://www.itl.nist.gov/iad/humanid/feret/. Accessed March 15, 2010.

[9]   A. Mascher-Kampfer, H. Stögner. and A. Uhl. Comparison of Compression Algorithms' Impact on Fingerprint and Face Recognition Accuracy. In *Proceedings of the SPIE*, volume 6508, pages 650810.1-650810.12, 2007.

[10]   T. Bourlai, and J. Kittler, and K. Messer. JPEG Compression Effects on Smart Card Face Verification System. In *Conference on Machine Vision Applications*, pages 426-429, May 2005.

[11]   National Institute of Standards and Technology. 2010. Special Database 32 – Multiple Encounter Dataset I (MEDS-I). Edited by C. Watson, S. Curry, D. Founds, J. Marques, and N. Orlans. Accessed 2010-02-14 at http://www.nist.gov/itl/iad/ig/sd32.cfm.

[12]   P. Hennings-Yeomans, S. Backer, and B. Kumar. Recognition of Low-Resolution Faces Using Multiple Still Images and Multiple Cameras. In *Biometrics: Theory, Applications and Systems, 2008.* BTAS September, 2008.

[13]   S. Lee, J. Park, and S. Lee. Low Resolution Face Recognition Based on Support Vector Data Description. In *Pattern Recognition.* Volume 39, issue 9. Pages 1809-1812, September 2006.

[14]   H. Han, S. Shan, X. Chen, and W. Gao. Gray-scale Super-resolution for Face Recognition from Low Gray-scale Resolution Face Images. In *17th IEEE International Conference on Image Processing (ICIP).* Pages 2825-2828, September 2008.

[15]   B. Li, H. Chang, S. Shan, and X. Chen. Low-Resolution Face Recognition via Coupled Locality Preserving Mappings. In *Signal Processing Letters, IEEE.* Volume 17, issue 1. Pages 20-23, 2010.

[16]   J. Zeb. Low Resolution Single Neural Network Based Face Recognition. In *4th International Conference on Computer Vision, Image and Signal Processing (CISP 07).* 2007.

[17]   K. Linga, R. Babu, L. Kishore, L. Agarwal, and M. Maanasa. Face Recognition Based on Multi Scale Low Resolution Feature Extraction and Single Neural Network. In *International Journal of Computer Science and Network Security.* Volume 8, Number 6, June 2008.

[18]   Independent JPEG Group. libjpeg 8. Retrieved from http://www.ijg.org/. Accessed February 14, 2011.

[19]   M. Figueroa-Villanueva, N. Ratha, and R. Bolle. A Comparative Performance Analysis of JPEG 2000 vs. WSQ for Fingerprint Image Compression. *Lecture Notes in Computer Science*, volume 2688, pages 385-392, 2003.

[20]   P. Grother, E. Tabassi, G. Quinn, W. Salamon. IREX I: Performance of Iris Recognition Algorithms on Standard Images. Technical Report. National Institute of Standards and Technology, October 2009. Published as NIST Interagency Report 7629.

[21]   F. Ebrahimi, M. Chamik, and S. Winlker. JPEG vs. JPEG2000: An Objective Comparison of Image Encoding Quality. In *Proceedings of SPIE Applications of Digital Image Processing.* Pages 300-308, 2004.

[22]   M. D. Adams, and F. Kossentini. JasPer: a software-based JPEG-2000 codec implementation. In *Proceedings of the International Conference on Image Processing, 2000.* Volume 2, pages 53-56, 2000.

[23]   National Television System Committee (NTSC) color television standard. December, 1953.

[24]   G. Doddington, W. Liggett, A. Martin, M. Przybocki, and D. Reynolds. Sheep, Goats, Lambs and Wolves: A Statistical Analysis of Speaker Performance in the NIST 1998 Speaker Recognition Evaluation. In *International Conference on Spoken Language Processing (ICSLP).* Sydney, 1998.

[25]   J. Nelder, and R. Mead. A Simplex Method for Function Minimization. In *The Computer Journal.* Pages 308-313, 1965.